Redware
America's Folk Art Pottery

Kevin McConnell

West Chester, Pennsylvania 19380

Beautifully slip-decorated bowl, probably 18th century; age lines and rim wear. 12" diameter, 4½" deep. Value: $90.00-$130.00.

Title page photo:
Heavily slip-decorated bowl, probably late 18th century. The age as well as the vivid subject matter make examples such as this one particularly valuable. 3¼"high, 9⅞" diameter. Value: $450.00-$600.00

Copyright © 1988 by Kevin McConnell.
Library of Congress Catalog Number: 88-64156.

Printed in the United States of America.
ISBN: 0-88740-159-7
Published by Schiffer Publishing Ltd.
1469 Morstein Road, West Chester, Pennsylvania 19380

This book may be purchased from the publisher.
Please include $2.00 postage.
Try your bookstore first.

Contents

Two miniature advertising beanpots (1½'' high. Value: $18.00-$25.00 each) and a tiny embossed jar (1'' high. Value: $10.00-$15.00).

Plate *sgraffito* decorated with stylized tulips, dated "1815" at top left. 11¾"
diameter. Examples of sgraffito such as this are among the rarest and most
sought after of all redware items. Value: $1800.00-$2200.00+. (Courtesy of
Landis Valley Museum.)

Large plate with coggled edge, *sgraffito* decorated flowers, and spectacular
copper oxide splashes. Note that this plate is dated "1819" at the top center.
11⅞" diameter. Value: $1800.00-$2200.00+. (Courtesy of Landis Valley
Museum.)

4

Acknowledgements
Contributing Collectors, Shops, and Museums

If you collect antiques, then you already know that the hobby is comprised of an awful lot of very kind and accommodating folks. This fact was reaffirmed time and again during the course of my work on this book, as people I'd never met before led me into their homes or shops and trusted me with their redwares. Without their generosity this book quite simply would not exist, and this is my small way of saying "thank you" to those who helped...

Pennsylvania: John & Kathy Dangelo, Tom DeLong, James Goodling, Sweetie Harris, Heritage Antique Mall, John & Marilyn Kubalak, Lancaster County Antique & Collectible Market, Landis Valley Farm Museum, Mr. & Mrs. C.H. McConnell, Dave & Violet Ristau, Peter & Nancy Schiffer, John R. & Lane Snedden, Craig Taylor, Betsi Yerkes, and Zettle's Antiques.

New York State: Chataqua Antiques, Danielson Antiques, The Farm Bell, The Marketplace on Main, Militello Antiques, Mrs. Evelyn Norberg, Olean Antique Center, Stockton Sales, and Mrs. Joyce Wight.

North Texas: Antique Crossroads Mall, Antiques Etc., John Bennett, Burleson Antique Mall, Bob & Georgia Caraway,

Cleburne Antique Mall, Greenberg-Pearlman Antiques, Bob Gordon, Robert Newton, and Patrick Rankin.

And Special Thanks To:

Kyle Husfloen, Editor of *The Antique Trader Weekly* and Frances L. Graham of *Antique & Collecting Hobbies* for allowing me to use material which has previously appeared in their respective publications.

John Lewis, photo consultant.

Marilyn Kubalak, additional photographs.

Maria Campbell-Brent, illustrations.

And last but not least, good old Mom and Dad for all of their help and understanding on this endeavor.

English black-glazed redware teapot with lustre highlighting. 8" high, 8½" long. Value: $125.00-$175.00.

Introduction
Redware Ramblings and Observations

Four thousand miles, two hundred photos, and innumerable hours later, the long and winding journey that is this book comes to a wheezing, grinding halt. And now that it's all said and done, I must tell you that it's been a most singular learning experience and adventure.

When I first set out to write and photograph this book several months ago, I thought that I possessed a rather complete understanding of redware and that I would encounter relatively few surprises. Boy, was I wrong.

During the weeks that I photographed redware collections, I was surprised, astounded, and awed on an almost daily basis. Consequently, my appreciation and enthusiasm for redware has taken on whole new vistas.

One important thing that I've come to realize about redware is that these fragile pieces of pottery provide us with an integral

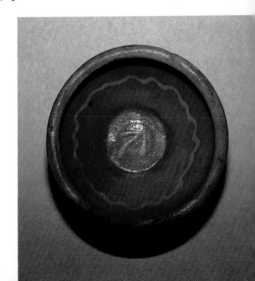

Small slip-decorated bowl. 2" high, 4½" diameter. Value: $70.00-$90.00.

link to the past. Indeed, for those who are willing to take the time to look and listen, redware can tell us many things about the life and times of the early American settlers. Redware is pioneer pottery, and the hands that shaped redware also helped to shape this nation's history.

In an effort to convey to you the warmth and diversity that is redware pottery, you will find this book to contain a minimum of text and a maximum of photos. With a subject such as redware, I am of the humble opinion that nothing informs and educates quite as well as a whole bunch of photographs. I think you'll agree.

Within these pages, I've attempted to represent most of the major redware forms that were made, with an emphasis on the kind of items that you're more inclined to see or own. Like myself, I suspect that you will be amazed by the great variety of shapes and colors that this ware offers.

In closing, I can't help but wonder how the redware potters of old would react to learn that their efforts are today collected and coveted by legions of primitive pottery afficianados. I'd like to think that they'd be pleased and flattered to discover that their descendants think so highly of their workmanship and have preserved it accordingly.

Enjoy.

Coarse-bodied ovoid jug with heavy green "tobacco spit" or alkaline glaze. Attributed to North Carolina. 15" high. Value: $120.00-$150.00

Pricing

What It All Means

In all honesty, the most difficult part of producing this book was not: driving 26 hours nonstop from Texas to Pennsylvania; nor was it a veritable gauntlet of bad weather: and it wasn't running out of gas in the mountains of Pennsylvania; and neither was it trying to take outdoor photos in the midst of a winter thunderstorm.

No indeed, for me, the trickiest and most daunting portion of this book was trying to come up with a more or less consistent, realistic price scheme for the approximately two hundred redware items pictured herein.

In an effort to do just that, I consulted numerous current price guides, and took into account auction figures and antique store prices. From these various sources I came up with average retail price ranges that I believe to reflect current redware values.

Nevertheless, this is just a guide of sorts, and no one should feel particularly obligated to charge or to pay the prices that I've set forth. Despite its age and fragility, redware abounds and many bargains yet exist for those who are willing to look and persevere.

It is my hope that this book will help to familiarize you, the collector, with the many different redware objects that were made and that by learning what they're worth, you'll be able to use your knowledge to seek out good buys accordingly.

4¾" high jug bank. Value: $55.00-$75.00.

Folk art mug with colorful incised scene, probably late 19th century. 3¼" high. Value: $120.00-$150.00.

A Word About Condition

At the risk of stating the obvious: virtually all antique redware was made well over a century ago, was very fragile and impractible, but nonetheless was intended for utilitarian purposes. Because of this, most redware objects you see will evidence honest use and wear such as chips, roughage, or even a hairline crack. Do not let such defects prevent you from purchasing a redware item. They are an inescapable fact of the ware or the nature of the beast if you will. Such wear should be looked upon as a part of the authentic charm of an old and primitive ceramic type.

The prices quoted in this book are for redware items with typical wear and tear. Authentic antique redware objects in mint condition are, of course, worth a premium.

An example of Quimper pottery, a traditional French folk art ware often made from red clay. 6½" diameter. Value: $35.00-$45.00.

Lidded milk pitcher slip decorated and dated "1883". Although late 19th century the intricate slip work, the date, and the matching lid combine to make this an attractive and valuable item. 6⅛" high. Value: $110.00-$140.00.

Highly unusual tree-form pitcher with elaborate detailing. 10¼" high. Value: $175.00-$210.00.

12

Redware Terminology

Jugtown Pottery: Located in Moore County, North Carolina this pottery has made traditional primitive-type redware and stoneware items since the 1920s. Jugtown wares are always potter's marked as such.

Lead Glazed: The clear, glassy glaze typically found on most redware items. Since redware is very porous, this glaze was utilized to render pieces waterproof.

Ovoid: This refers to the pear-shaped, squat bodies of jugs, jars, and crocks that were made prior to 1830.

Oxides: Powdered mineral compositions used to color, high-light, or decorate redware objects. Copper - green, iron oxide - brown, manganese - mirror black.

Quimper: Traditional French folk art pottery often made from redware clay. Quimper has been made in the same style for centuries and continues to be manufactured today. Items made since 1926 are marked "Henriot Quimper".

Redware: European or early American pottery generally of the utilitarian type made from clay containing iron mineral compounds, which fired to a reddish hue in the kiln.

Sgraffito: A specialized, highly valuable redware variant made predominantly by 19th century Pennsylvania Germans. This technique involved slipping, incising, and oxide decorating

Bulldog figurine, probably a doorstep or mantle ornament. 7" high. Value: $150.00-$200.00.

redware items with beautiful and often complex designs and scenes.

Slip-Decorated/Slipware: A technique by which redware objects were coated or decorated with liquid clays of contrasting color. A device known as a slip cup was often used, which functioned similar to a funnel. Slip cups often had several openings and were used to trace quick but complex linear designs on plates and platters.

Wire-Cut Base: This refers to the "fingerprint-like" pattern left on the bottom of redware objects which were cut from the potter's wheel with a length of wire.

Wheel Thrown: The method by which much redware pottery was made, involving a foot operated potter's wheel which when operated at 100 revolutions per minute allowed the potter to shape the raw redware clay into the requisite form.

Handled bottle with slip decoration, probably European. 11" high. Value: $250.00-$300.00.

Redware Rarity Chart

The following charts will help you to determine at a glance the potential value and rarity of almost any redware item...

Group One/Most Common:

Undecorated utilitarian objects such as jugs, bowls, jars, bean pots, food molds, pitchers, bottles, pie plates, crocks, chamber pots, and churns, as well as spittoons, chicken waterers, pipe bowls, and most miniatures (bean pots, pitchers, etc.).

Group Two/ Relatively Rare:

Plates, bowls, and other items slip-decorated with simple designs, vases, flasks, inkwells, collanders, figurines, banks, small tea pots, flower pots, pepper shakers, rundlets or canteens, face jugs, water coolers, candlesticks, objects decorated with embossed or applied designs, and unusual miniatures (food molds, spittoons, churns, etc.).

Small redware jug with applied handle and unglazed exterior. 7¼" high. Value: $55.00-$70.00.

Group Three/Very Rare & Valuable:

Any examples of sgraffito, examples of slipware with names, dates, or folk sayings, objects decorated with Pennsylvania Dutch motifs, large, fancy urns, jardinieres, or vases, pitcher and basin sets, loaf dishes, bird-shaped whistles, large and elaborate tea pots.

Cylidrical tankard with strap handle and shiny glaze. 10" high. Value: $95.00-$120.00.

Black glazed ovoid jar. Note the Pennsylvania Dutch hex signs embossed at base of handles. 8" high. Value: $250.00-$325.00.

Collecting Redware Pottery

A Brief History of Manufacture and Usage

When we look at red clay bricks, flower pots, and terra cotta roof and floor tiles, what we are actually seeing are the last vestiges of a redware industry that once thrived in America and in Europe for centuries.

Perhaps more than any other ceramic type, redware enjoys the longest and the most complicated history of manufacture and utilization.

Consider that when prehistoric American Indians first fashioned their crude pottery vessels over three thousand years ago, they were making use of redware clay to do so. Likewise, the ancient Egyptians, Greeks, and Romans formed red clay into myriad artistic and utilitarian shapes.

Indeed, natural deposits of redware clay can be found worldwide and were exploited by man in some fashion since the very beginning. It would not be unreasonable to suggest that the

Object on left with flared mouth is a "spit cup" or spittoon (4¼" high, Value: $140.00-$180.00.) while the object on the right is a small mug or cup (3" high, Value: $70.00-$90.00).

making and usage of redware pottery played a part in every major culture throughout time.

However, for our specific purposes, it is necessary to limit our focus largely to that which was produced in Colonial/Early America. Of course, it is only logical that the redware made by Colonists was both an extension and a continuation of a ceramic tradition rooted in Europe.

Therefore, it must be noted that the French turned out a type of country redware known as terre jaspe (or red earth) from the mid-sixteenth century on up through the nineteenth century. In England, various red clay wares were also manufactured, the most pertinent being slip-decorated redwares which enjoyed great popularity and were produced in quantity by various Staffordshire potteries during the latter seventeenth century and on into the eighteenth.

Redware was the first pottery made in Colonial America, and its production certainly began almost as soon as the settlers arrived. In fact, there is firm archeological evidence to show that attractive, well-formed wares were made at the Jamestown Island, Virginia Colony by trained potters as early as 1625.

The motivations of these Colonists are not too difficult to speculate upon, for they needed a functional, inexpensive ware to supplement their pewter and wooden commodities.

It only made sense that they would choose redware, for these surface clays are both abundant and easily accesible in the area they occupied. It was also relatively simple to make, since the ware

Soup bowls with clear interior glaze. 6½" diameter. Value: $50.00-$70.00 each.

Left: jar with elaborate black sponging. 6'' high. Value: $200.00-$250.00.
Right: ovoid jar with black daubing. 8½'' high. Value: $225.00-$300.00.

Unusual and possibly unique footbath with lug handles and yellow striping.
22'' long, 15½'' wide. Value: $425.00-$500.00.

The 19th century redware potter at work. Note the construction of the potter's wheel. Illustration by Maria Campbell Brent.

Two wide-mouthed preserve jars. Left: 4½'' high, right: 3½'' high. Value: Jar on left: $110.00-$130.00 due to unusual glaze. jar on right: $30.00-$50.00.

could be fired at a low temperature (between 1600 and 1800 degrees Farenheit) in a small, crude kiln.

To aid in understanding, the step by step process by which redware was made is as follows. The desired clay was dug by hand and then allowed to weather over the course of a winter, which tended to improve the plasticity of the material.

Said clay was then cleaned of impurities in a small horsepowered mill, at which time it was removed and kneaded by hand to remove any air pockets which would otherwise explode in the heated kiln.

At this stage, the clay was ready to be shaped by the potter, either being crudely molded by hand or formed on a foot-powered potter's wheel. The basic potter's wheel consisted of a wooden or metal disk attached to the top of a long rod. Affixed to the base of the rod was a heavy stone wheel which the potter would kick thus revolving the entire assemblage which was usually mounted onto a work table. Approximately one hundred revolutions per minute were required in order for the potter to be able to give the raw clay form.

After being made, the objects were allowed to dry for three or four weeks to permit for the removal of moisture from the clay prior to being fired in the kiln.

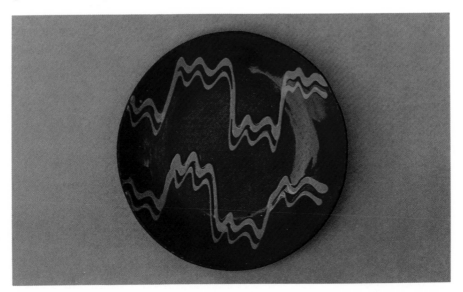

Plate with coggled edge and wavy yellow slip. 6⅞" diameter. Value: $150.00-$190.00.

Chicken waterer. 5" high. $20.00-$30.00.

At best, the firing of the kiln was a problematic process which relied as much on luck as it did skill. Utilizing wood for fuel, it was necessary to maintain an approximate temperature of 1800 degrees Farenheit in the kiln for a period of thirty to thirty-six hours. There was a great deal of guess-work involved as well as failures and disasters, since the potter could not open the kiln to examine his wares until it had cooled down.

The things they made consisted of a few basic utilitarian forms such as pitchers, crocks, and milk basins. The interiors were rendered waterproof through the use of a clear lead glaze, made from a mixture of powdered red lead, clay, fine sand, and water.

With the arrival of more and more Colonists in the New World, some of whom were skilled potters, the types and variety of redware were to change with the passage of time. Where before only a few basic forms were made, more people and more needs gave advent to a large spectrum of redware objects which included everything from inkwells to flowerpots to children's toys.

Additionally, the mass production of slipware or slipped redware in England resulted in it being manufactured by potters in Colonial America. Quite simply, slipware is a redware object which has been decorated (or covered) through the application of a different colored clay; this decoration running the range from a few squiggly lines, to a clever folk saying, to depictions of birds and flowers.

Dome shaped bank with incised decor. Base is incised "FWS, 1867". 4⅞" high. Value: $320.00-$350.00.

Bank Base.

Nicely shaped jar, possibly a humidor. 6¾" high. Value: $45.00-$60.00.

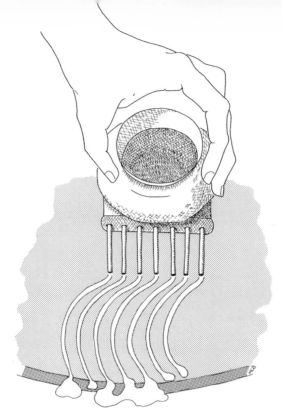

The slip cup in use. Such cups were usually made out of fired redware clay and fitted with hollow turkey quills through which the slip flowed. Illustration by Maria Campbell Brent.

Unglazed bean pot with lid and strap handle. 6¾" high. Value: $40.00-$60.00.

To further explain, the clay slip was the consistency of buttermilk, and the potter applied it through the use of a tool known as a slip cup. This instrument can be likened to a funnel, having anywhere from one to four spouts (often made from hollow turkey quills), the flow from which the skilled artisan controlled with his fingers. After being slip-decorated, the redware object was fired in the kiln, thus making the designs on the surface a permanent part of it. Note that the slip was usually made from whitish-yellow pipe clay that was imported from England.

But it was the people of German descent who settled in Pennsylvania that elevated redware from a utilitarian household ceramic to objects of artistic virtue. These people produced a beautiful redware variant referred to as *sgraffito* (meaning to scratch). Although widely credited with inventing the *sgraffito* technique, it is important to clarify that the Pennsylvania Germans actually revived and repopularized it as it was practiced in England during the seventeenth century.

Sgraffito was made by coating a redware plate or platter with a yellowish slip which was allowed to semi-dry. At this point, the maker would begin to scratch through the paste-like slip with a sharp tool, revealing the red clay body beneath in beautiful contrast.

Bean pot with spectacular glaze and incised Pennsylvania Dutch motifs. 6½" high. Value: $450.00-$600.00.

Preserve jars. Left: 9" high, Value: $30.00-$40.00. Right: 7" high, Value: $50.00-$70.00. The presence of a lid adds to the value and desirability of an item.

Using this technique, he would intricately incise the object with complex geometric designs, detailed folk scenes, and even names and dates. Often, the designs were further highlighted by outlining them with the application of colorful mineral oxides.

Since existing pieces of *sgraffito* exhibit little or no use and wear, it is thought that they were in all likelihood made as gifts for special events and were much treasured by the recipient. Well over a century later, such pieces are still prized and held in high esteem as ultimate examples of folk art.

Although during the late eighteenth and on into the nineteenth century redware was mass-produced by several East Coast potteries (such as the Norton pottery of Bennington, Vermont), this ware by and large remained the domain of the small, country potter As a result, it retains more of a folk charm than many other antique ceramic types.

Redware remained a viable mainstay ceramic for the Colonists and Early Americans from the 1600s into the 1800s. Nonetheless, redware was not without its faults and production of it began to wane by 1800. It had all but ceased except to a small degree in some areas of Pennsylvania, Virginia, Illinois, and North Carolina, where production persisted as late as 1900.

Canning jar with greenish-amber glaze and orange flecks. 7'' high. Value: $75.00-$95.00.

Several factors contributed to the demise of the redware industry in this country, the most obvious being the inherent fragility of the ware. While it was relatively easy and inexpensive to make, it was also prone to breakage due to the coarseness of the ware, the low temperature at which it was fired, and the soft lead glaze covering it.

The discovery of durable stoneware and brownware clays in America coupled with the commercial production and transportation of them led to the end for redware. In addition to the discovery of redware's poisonous lead glaze, the advent of the glass canning jar, the invention of the ice box, and the importation of inexpensive whitewares all served to render it forever obsolete.

It's interesting to note that by 1800 it was common knowledge that the lead glaze used on redware was highly toxic, but in spite of this health hazard it continued to be made and used for many more decades until cheaper wares replaced it. Consequently, it was economic rather than health factors that terminated redware production.

Now many decades later, redware has made a comeback - this time with collectors of country ceramics, folk art, and Americana. For those interested in starting a collection of redware, there are

Jugtown pottery lidded redware bowl (with wooden ladle). 9" high, 10" diameter. Value: $40.00-$60.00.

several additional points worth remembering.

One is that redware gets its name from the fact that it was made from clay containing iron mineral compounds. As a result, when this clay was fired in the kiln, it took upon a reddish hue. Although many pieces were completely covered with colored glazes or slips ranging from green (copper oxide) to whitish-yellow (pipe clay) to black (manganese) to brown (iron salts), the unglazed base of an object will invariably reveal the true clay color to the diligent collector.

When considering a purchase, know that in terms of rarity and value, redware jugs are the most common and easiest to find, followed by bowls, jars, crocks, and beanpots. Among the more difficult objects to locate are vases, toys, flasks, inkwells and examples of *sgraffito*. Without a doubt, the best buys to be found by novice collectors at this time are the simple, undecorated utilitarian objects such as bowls and jars which have either a clear lead or shiny black manganese glaze. These items were made in vast quantities and are as yet still very much available and affordable.

Redware toys tend to be particularly elusive. Since the seventeenth century such items as whistles, miniature tea sets, flutes, and tops were made in America, but because of their fragility, precious few have survived the ravages of time and play and as a consequence are now quite expensive.

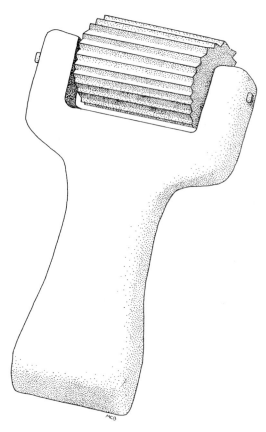

This tool is known as a coggling wheel and it was used to serrate the edges of plates and platters by running it along the edges of the unfired clay objects. Illustration by Maria Campbell Brent.

Jar with black glaze and unusual handles. 9¼'' high. Value: $200.00-$275.00.

Handled jar or urn with heavy green glaze. 9¾'' high. Value: $140.00-$185.00.

In addition to rarity of form, the presence of decoration is also a value factor. Simply put, a decorated piece is more valuable than a plain one, and the more elaborate or unusual the design work (as with a *sgraffito* plate), the more desirable and expensive the redware object.

Likewise, potter-marked pieces are worth a premium and should be looked for; among some of the more notable American redware manufacturers whose products often bear a die-impressed mark are those made by: John Bell of Waynesboro, Pennsylvania, Alvin Wilcox of West Bloomfield, New York, and Lorenzo Johnson of Newstead, New York. Rarely found, the presence of a potter's mark will greatly enhance the value of any redware item.

Insofar as the question of authenticity goes, truly antique redware items (excepting *sgraffito)* were heavily used by their owners and will consequently show telltale signs of age and utilization, such as small chips, hairline cracks, and basal wear. Also be aware that the majority of old redware items have unglazed bases due to the glazing and firing techniques employed during that early period.

Two small preserve jars with lead-glazed interiors. 4½"-5" high. Value: $25.00-$35.00.

Another feature useful in identifying and authenticating antique redware items is the following. Those redware objects made on a potter's wheel were removed from it through the use of a length of fine wire which was worked back and forth near the base of the item until it completely cut through the soft clay, thus severing it from the wheel. This crude process left a series of cuts upon the base of the redware item resembling a giant fingerprint which became a permanent part of the base once it was fired in the kiln.

Probably the greatest bewilderment facing collectors of antique redware is the inability to distinguish American-made pieces from imported European redwares. Since both products were part of the same pottery-making tradition and one tended to more or less emulate the other, categorization by country is in most cases a matter of conjecture.

Additionally, specific dating of redware objects is very difficult since many of the basic utilitarian forms remained largely unchanged throughout the duration of manufacture. Consequently, trying to distinguish a redware bowl made in 1750 from one made in 1830 would be out of the question since they would be almost identical in every way.

It is however possible to establish relative dates for redware storage vessels such as jugs and jars. Those made prior to 1830 will evidence ovoid or pear-shaped bodies, while those made after 1830

Black glazed storage jar. 7¼" high.
Value: $60.00-$75.00.

will be straight-sided in form. But for the most part, redware collectors must content themselves with the general knowledge that their items are truly antiques and are well-made and decorated.

One possible exception that might confuse the beginning collector would be the redware products of the Jugtown Pottery. This pottery has operated from the 1920s to the present day in Moore County, North Carolina, producing such traditional country ceramics as those discussed in this article.

Redware clay is often used by Jugtown, and while these pieces are not truly antiques, they are nevertheless quite collectible and could make desirable additions to any redware assemblage. Such items are always clearly marked "Jugtown Ware" on the bottom.

Collectors likewise need to know that in addition to Jugtown, there is currently a "redware renaissance" under way in this country. Modern day potters who are skilled folk artists in their own right are currently making a wide array of traditional redware objects.

Obviously recognizable as being new, it is a matter of personal preference as to whether one wishes to add contemporary pieces to their collection. In any case, it is important to be aware that they do exist and that the redware-making tradition continues on.

In general, it would behoove any collector to further their knowledge of redware by reading available literature on the subject (see bibliography) as well as studying examples displayed in museums or antique shops. Remember, the greater your knowledge of a ware, the better chance you have of making a good buy.

On that note, it is necessary to add that excellent redware bargains can still be found in the United States and in England. It has been the author's experience that many dealers and auctioneers seem to be unaware of what redware is or of its value, and often it is mistaken for dirty stoneware and can be purchased quite reasonably.

As detailed, the redware pottery tradition has spanned many centuries; as a result there are plenty of examples of this folk material culture for collectors to discover and enjoy. Good luck and good hunting.

Kevin McConnell
Denton, Texas

Late 19th/early 20th century piggy bank with red clay body and heavy marbleized glaze. Probably made in Austria. 4¼" long. Value: $40.00-$65.00.

Bowls and Plates

Side view of milk cooling basin/bowl with clear lead glaze. 5⅞" high, 15" diameter. Value: $75.00-$125.00.

Top view of milk cooling basin.

Lead-glazed pie plate. 9½'' diameter. Value: $50.00-$70.00.

Slip-decorated bowl with scrollwork and squiggles. 3 ½'' high, 8¾'' diameter. Value: $175.00-$230.00.

Reverse side of slipware plate reveals both wear and tooling marks.

Large slip-decorated charger. 16¼'' diameter. Value: $295.00-$350.00.

Pie plate with coggled edge and dark brown glaze. 9¾'' diameter. $60.00-$85.00.

Undecorated plate with dark brown glaze. 7'' diameter. Value: $35.00-$50.00.

Large bowl with textured interior. 15½'' diameter. Value: $100.00-$140.00.

Bowl with green glaze and orange speckling. 4'' high, 7'' diameter. Value: $70.00-$85.00.

Large slipware bowl. 13¾" diameter. Value: $400.00-$450.00.

Elaborate slip-decorated bowl with flowers and name. 10" diameter. Value: $500.00-$550.00.

Large milk bowl with yellow interior slip. 10" diameter, 9½" deep. Value: $300.00-$350.00.

Large relief-molded bowl with black splashes. 10½" diameter, 3" deep. Value: $300.00-$360.00.

Bowl with brown interior sponging. 11" diameter, 5" deep. Value: $250.00-$285.00.

Bowl with pour spout. Side view. 9½" diameter. Value: $75.00-$90.00.

Slip decorated bowl. 6⅞" diameter, 3" deep. Value: $150.00-$175.00.

Undecorated milk bowl. 9½" diameter, 3½" deep. Value: $70.00-$90.00.

Large bowl with applied lug handles and clear interior glaze. 16" diameter, 6½" deep. Value: $120.00-$160.00.

Large vegetable or loaf dish with marbleized glaze. 11¼" long, 9" wide. Value: $550.00-$700.00.

Slipware bowl, dated "1823". 10" diameter. Value: $600.00-$800.00+.

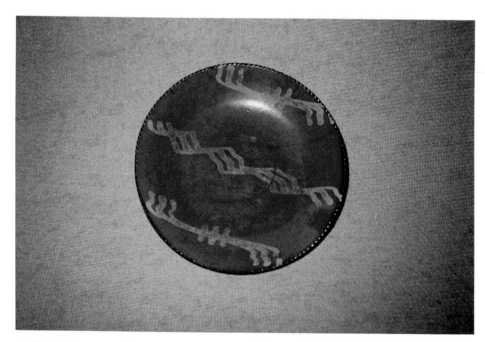

Plate with coggled edge and yellow slip decor. 9¾" diameter. Value: $160.00-$200.00.

Slip-decorated plate. Some interior wear and damage. 8⅞" diameter. Value: $120.00-$150.00.

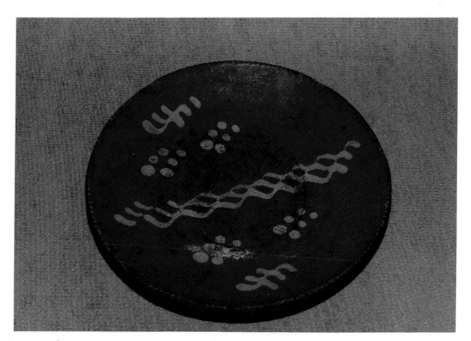

Plate with coggled rim and varied slip decorated designs. 10 ½" diameter. Value: $350.00-$400.00.

Large and highly unusual plate slip-decorated as follows: "JM Shaw, Housepainter, paper hanger, etc., Quakertown, Bucks County, Penn." Elaborate examples of slipware like this are very rare and very valuable. 13" diameter. Value: $1300.00-$1800.00+. (Courtesy of Landis Valley Museum.)

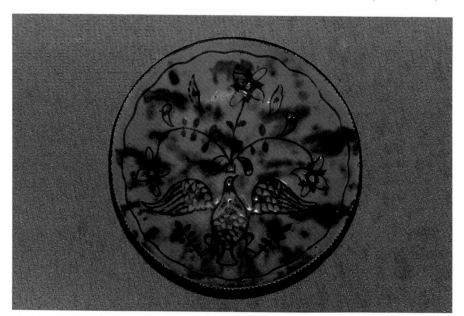

Plate sgraffito decorated with eagle, flowers, and vines, and highlighted with brown and green oxide splashes. 8⅞" diameter. Attributed to the potter Meddinger. Value: $800.00-$1100.00. (Courtesy of Landis Valley Museum.)

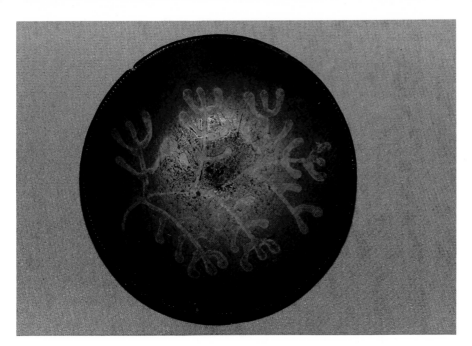

Plate slip-decorated with "tree of life" pattern. 11 ¼" diameter. Value: $375.00-$425.00. (Courtesy of Landis Valley Museum.)

Large slip-decorated plate or charger. 14½" diameter. Value: $350.00-$450.00. (Courtesy of Landis Valley Museum.)

Obverse and reverse of a Jugtown Pottery plate with vivid pumpkin and oxide coloration. Note potter's mark on plate base. 9'' diameter. Value: $45.00-$65.00.

Grotesque redware plate, tooled and incised flower form with heavy black manganese glaze. Back side is incised "Dec. 4th, 1868." 7½" diameter. Value: $150.00-$200.00. (Courtesy of Landis Valley Museum.)

Jars, Crocks and Churns

Two gallon crock with applied ear handles and slip-dated "1830" near the base. The presence of a date is unusual and adds greatly to the value of any redware object. 8½" high, 9½" diameter. Value: $225.00-$300.00.

Unglazed base of crock clearly shows the redware clay it was made from.

Large ovoid storage jar. The bulbous shape of this specimin suggests that it was made prior to 1830. 15¼'' high. Value: $125.00-$180.00. The exceptional size, shape, and condition makes this a valuable piece.

Unglazed red clay mustard jar with detailed transfer print hunting scene. English registry mark on the base provides an exact date of 1856. 4¼" high. Value: $40.00-$55.00.

Black manganese glazed preserve jar. 6⅛" high. Value: $40.00-$60.00.

Squat, ear-handled storage jar. 8" high. Value: $30.00-$50.00.

Apple butter or preserve jar, 7" high, 8½" diameter at mouth. Value: $30.00-$45.00.

Base of preserve jar clearly shows marks designating that it was cut off of the potter's wheel with a piece of wire after having been formed.

Back side of four gallon churn shows areas of thick brownish-green glaze.

Large ovoid four gallon churn with applied ear handles. Incised "4" evident near the top. 16½" high. Value: $140.00-$200.00.

Preserve jar with black manganese glaze. 6½" high. Value: $40.00-$60.00.

Small preserve or apple butter jar with unglazed exterior. 3½'' high. Value: $25.00-$35.00.

Ovoid, ear-handled storage jar or milk crock. Made prior to 1830. 12'' high. Value: $70.00-$95.00.

Large interior glazed pot or basin. 6¾'' high, 9'' diameter. Value: $60.00-$80.00.

Large ear-handled jar or churn, with partial glaze and incised "5" near rim. 18'' high. Value: $180.00-$220.00.

Preserve jar, orange glaze with black manganese splashes. 8" high. Value: $60.00-$75.00.

Squat, black glazed preserve or canning jar. 5" high. Value: $45.00-$60.00.

Squat creamer with yellow glaze and brown sponging. 2½" high. Value: $90.00-$110.00.

Lidded jar with black glaze. 9¼" high. Value: $75.00-$95.00.

Handled preserve jar with brown sponging. 5½" high. Value: $150.00-$180.00.
Storage jar with incised lines. 9" high. Value: $75.00-$95.00.

Preserve jar with unusual checker-board decor. 9¼" high. Value: $75.00-$95.00.

Large storage jar with black glaze and fancy applied handles. 11½" high. Value: $175.00-$225.00.

Lidded jar with yellow glaze. 6½'' high. Value: $90.00-$110.00.

Ovoid spice jar with lid. 11'' high. Value: $90.00-$120.00.

Ovoid, ear-handled storage jar. 9½'' high. Value: $45.00-$65.00.

Jugs, Bottles, Bean Pots and Molds

Unusual food mold with dark brown glaze. 3½'' high, 5'' diameter. Value: $70.00-$90.00.

Food mold with fancy slip decor. 3¾'' high, 5½'' diameter. Value: $65.00-$85.00.

A 20th century Jugtown ware jug, 4⅞'' high. Value: $30.00-$45.00.

The die-impressed potter's mark which appears on the products of all Jugtown ware.

Bean pot with clear lead glaze. 6'' high. Value: $35.00-$50.00.

Base of bean pot evidences extensive use and wear so characteristic of early earthenware.

Large handleless bean pot with incised shoulder, unglazed exterior, lead-glazed interior. 6¼'' high. Value: $40.00-$50.00.

Handled jug with dark brown glaze. The perpendicular rather than ovoid sides of this piece indicates that it dates from the second half of the 19th century. 12¼'' high. Value: $40.00-$65.00.

Exterior view of a large Turk's head cake mold. Note the rich olive green (copper/lead) glaze as well as the applied ring to facilitate hanging. 4½" deep, 11" diameter. Value: $95.00-$135.00.

Interior view of the cake mold further exhibits the fine glaze, form, and condition of this piece.

Ovoid jug with clear lead glaze and applied strap handle. 7½" high. Value: $60.00-$80.00.

Cylindrical bottle with drab brown glaze. Late 19th century, possibly used for ginger beer. 5⅞" high. Value: $20.00-$35.00.

Known as either a rundlet, canteen, or keg, this 6" high container was once used to hold various liquids including water, rum, and whiskey. Notice the beautiful slip decoration as well as the oblate shape of this odd object. The two holes facilitate the outward flow of the liquid contents. This item generally dates from the first half of the 19th century. Value: $185.00-$240.00.

Partially glazed bean pot. Interior is fully glazed to retain liquids. 6" high.
Value: $40.00-$60.00.

Two gallon ovoid jug with brown/black glaze. 12" high. Value: $85.00-$105.00.

Late 19th century ginger beer bottle. 8½" high. Value: $20.00-$35.00.

Plain round mold. 8½'' diameter. Value: $55.00-$70.00.

"Turk's head" mold. 9'' diameter. Value: $65.00-$80.00.

Unusual octagonal mold with interior design. 6" long. 4¾" wide. Value: $95.00-$145.00.

A small flask or bottle with brown daubing. 4½" high. Value: $130.00-$175.00.

A large flask with black glaze. 7⅛" high. Value: $150.00-$200.00.

Rare and unusual hot water bottle. 10" diameter, 2⅞" high. Value: $250.00-$300.00.

Face jug/bottle. Antique pieces such as this one were traditionally made in the southern states by pre-emancipation slave potters. 9½" high. Value: $250.00-$325.00.

Ovoid jug with slip-decoration, probably European. Glaze flaking at top. 7⅞" high. Value: $85.00-$110.00.

Pitchers, Creamers, and Mugs

Mug, 3¾" high with applied strap handle and multicolored glaze. Value: $60.00-$85.00.

Large milk or pancake batter pitcher with applied strap handle and dark brown glaze. 9⅞" high. Value: $90.00-$125.00.

Creamer with bulbous bottom, dark brown glaze and applied handle. 2½" high. Value: $80.00-$95.00.

Mug with dark brownish-black glaze. 3⅛'' high. Value: $40.00-$60.00.

Sgraffito decorated creamer. European, late 19th century. 3⅛'' high. Value: $85.00-$100.00.

Relief-molded miniature mug. German late 19th century. 1⅞'' high. Value: $20.00-$25.00.

Miniature cup in the form of a child's head and face. 2¼'' high. Value: $40.00-$55.00.

Strap-handled mug or pot with unglazed exterior. 4'' high. Value: $30.00-$45.00.

Nicely shaped preserve jar or "corker" with black manganese glaze. 9¼" high. Value: $45.00-$65.00.

Strap handled pitcher with partial green glaze. Very unusual form. 9½" high. Value: $145.00-$175.00.

Strap handled mug with marbleized glaze. 3¾" high. Value: $70.00-$90.00.

Strap handled creamer with flared spout. 3'' high. Value: $95.00-$105.00.

Slipware pitcher and basin. Pitcher: 10½'' high, basin: 12½'' diameter. Value $900.00-$1000.00 set.

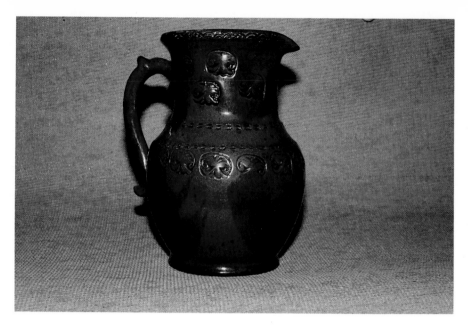

Beautifully decorated pitcher with fancy applied handle. 9" high. Value: $275.00-$350.00.

Bulbous pitcher with applied medallions and coggling. 8¼" high. Value: $250.00-$325.00.

Lidded pitcher with brown sponging. 6½" high. Value: $175.00-$250.00.

Handled mug with clear lead glaze, bulbous early form. 3⅛" high. Value: $150.00-$185.00.

Mug. 3" high. Early. Value: $70.00-$95.00.

Two mush cups with colorful glazes and exterior decor. Heavily worn. 4" high and 2¾" high. Value: $60.00-$80.00 each.

Pitcher with yellow slip highlighting. 7¼" high. Value: $100.00-$140.00.

Vases and Miniatures

A grouping of late 19th century unglazed redware miniatures. From left to right: a 2" high relief-molded ewer (value: $18.00-$25.00); a 1¾" high bean pot (value: $10.00-$15.00); and a 2⅛" high relief-molded figural whistle of a little girl holding a doll (value: $60.00-$75.00).

Miniature advertising bean pot, circa 1900. 2¼" high. Value: $15.00-$20.00.

Grotesque Chinaman figurine with heavy green copper oxide glaze. This unusual item may have functioned as a candleholder. 7¼" high. Value: $125.00-$175.00.

Top view of grotesque figurine; a true example of redware folk art.

Squat vase with green copper oxide glaze. Redware vases are rare to begin with and those with unusual glazes such as this example are highly desirable. 5½'' high. Value: $250.00-$325.00.

Waisted vase with crimped, tooled rim and colorful glaze. 6¾'' high. Value: $300.00-$375.00+.

Miniature plate, probably part of a child's tea set. 3¼'' diameter. Value: $10.00-$15.00.

Small vase with heavy white slip and blue sponging. 4½'' high. Value: $140.00-$180.00.

Miniature whimsey jugs. 3½''-4½'' high. Value: $20.00-$30.00 each.

Vase or goblet with white slip and blue sponging. 7¾'' high. Value: $240.00-$300.00.

Recumbent lion figurine. 5'' high, 8½'' diameter. Value: $95.00-$120.00.

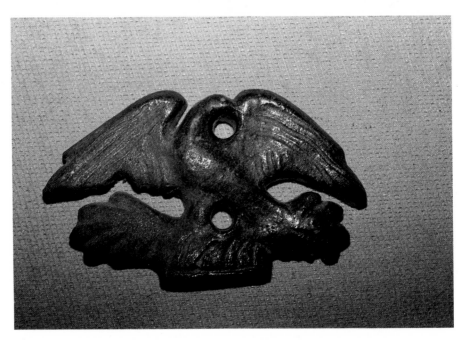

American eagle figurine. 9'' long. Value: $125.00-$155.00.

Relief-molded figural matchholder. Probably late 19th century. 8¼'' high.
Value: $95.00-$135.00.

A grouping of small redware items, including: a miniature yellow glazed mug (2½'' high, Value: $25.00-$35.00); an inkwell/bottle (2½'' high, Value: $20.00-$30.00); and a particularly primitive miniature mold (3½'' diameter, 1¼'' high, Value: $18.00-$25.00).

Small interior glazed bean pot. 2⅞'' high. Value: $14.00-$20.00.

Miniature pot with applied handles. 3¾'' high. Value: $30.00-$45.00.

Miniature molds. 2½'' and 3½'' diameter, 1½'' high. Value: $150.00-$185.00 each.

Miniature spittoon with black glaze. 3'' high. Value: $135.00-$160.00.

Miniature jug with excellent original paint. 2¼'' high. Value: $18.00-$25.00.

A grouping of miniatures, including: two "Turk's head" molds (3½" and 5½" diameter, Value: $160.00-$210.00 each) and a speckled bowl (3½" diameter, 1¼" high, Value: $40.00-$65.00).

Another grouping of redware including: A mortar (3½" diameter, 1½" high, Value: $65.00-$85.00) and two miniature jars (1¼" and 1½" high, Value: $15.00-$20.00 each).

Doll or figurine of a boy dressed in colonial attire; dark brown glaze. 3¼" high. Value: $95.00-$135.00.

Unglazed vase with flared rim and bulbous base. 7½" high. Value: $115.00-$145.00.

Unglazed vase with decorative beading. 6⅞" high. Value: $90.00-$120.00.

Oddities and Miscellanous

Red earthenware ocarina or "sweet potato". This quaint little musical instrument was very popular fron around 1860 to the turn of the century, with many of them having been made in Austria. 5⅛" long. Value: $20.00-$30.00.

Black glazed cuspidor. 4½" high. Value: $35.00-$45.00.

Handled chamber pot with yellow clay slip and green copper oxide flourishes. 5½'' high. Value: $90.00-$135.00.

Relief molded pipe bowls dating from the 19th century. 1½''-2½'' long. Value: $5.00-$10.00 each.

Strap-handled potty. 2⅞'' high, 5½'' diameter. Value: $45.00-$65.00.

Water cooler with incised initials and applied handles. 14½'' high. Value: $185.00-$240.00.

Pepper shaker with pewter top and fittings. 4'' high. Value: $85.00-$105.00.

Stove lift or pedestal for hot pans and dishes. 2¾'' high. Value: $18.00-$25.00.

Flower pot with multi-colored glaze. Heavy wear. 7⅞'' high. Value: $50.00-$80.00.

Bulbous bank with knob finial. 5¼'' high. Value: $65.00-$90.00.

Footed collander. 6'' high, 6¾'' diameter at top. Value: $200.00-$275.00.

Flower pot with attached saucer. Attributed to John Bell. 5½" high. Value: $190.00-$250-00.

Flower pot with saucer and tooled rim. Heavy wear. Value: $60.00-$80-00.

Large flower pot with saucer and tooled exterior. 9" high. Value: $120.00-$150.00.

Chicken waterer with coarse glaze. 6¼" high. Value: $25.00-$35.00.

Redware whimsey, possibly an early coin, token, or medallion. 1¾" diameter. Value: $20.00-$30.00.

Black-glazed teapot. 6½" high, 9¼" long. Value: $95.00-$125.00.

Primitive salt box. 5½" long, 2" deep. Value: $50.00-$75.00.

Footed master salt cellar/bowl; dark brown glaze with cream daubing. 2½" high, 4¾" diameter. Value: $135.00-$175.00.

Oversized cup and saucer (probably for soup or mush) with worn blue and white glaze. Saucer: 6½" diameter, cup: 5" diameter, overall height: 3½". Value: $90.00-$125.00.

Bibliography

Ian Bennett, *Book of American Antiques*

John L. Cotter & Paul J. Hudson, *New Discoveries at Jamestown*

Warren E. Cox, *The Book of Pottery and Porcelain*

Ivor Noel Hume, *A Guide to Artifacts of Colonial America*

William Ketchum, Jr., *Pottery and Porcelain*

Don and Carol Raycraft, *The Collector's Guide to Kitchen Antiques*

Albert Christian Revi, *The Spinning Wheel's Complete Book of Antiques*

George Savage & Harold Newman, *An Illustrated Dictionary of Ceramics*

Schroeder's Antiques Price Guide

Time-Life Books Encyclopedia of Collectibles

Warman's Antiques and their Prices

Alice Winchester, *The Antiques Book*